FACING YOUR FEARS

FACING YOUR FEAR OF MAKING NEW FRIENDS

BY RENEE BIERMANN

raintree
a Capstone company — publishers for children

Raintree is an imprint of Capstone Global Library Limited, a company incorporated in England and Wales having its registered office at 264 Banbury Road, Oxford, OX2 7DY – Registered company number: 6695582

www.raintree.co.uk
myorders@raintree.co.uk

Hardback edition text © Capstone Global Library Limited 2024
Paperback edition text © Capstone Global Library Limited 2025

The moral rights of the proprietor have been asserted. All rights reserved. No part of this publication may be reproduced in any form or by any means (including photocopying or storing it in any medium by electronic means and whether or not transiently or incidentally to some other use of this publication) without the written permission of the copyright owner, except in accordance with the provisions of the Copyright, Designs and Patents Act 1988 or under the terms of a licence issued by the Copyright Licensing Agency, 5th Floor, Shackleton House, 4 Battle Bridge Lane, London, SE1 2HX (www.cla.co.uk). Applications for the copyright owner's written permission should be addressed to the publisher.

Editorial credits
Editor: Erika L. Shores; Designer: Dina Her; Media Researcher: Jo Miller; Production Specialist: Tori Abraham

ISBN 978 1 3982 4997 4 (hardback)
ISBN 978 1 3982 4996 7 (paperback)

British Library Cataloguing in Publication Data
A full catalogue record for this book is available from the British Library.

Acknowledgements
Getty Images: Cavan Images, 19, Digital Vision., 5, FatCamera, 9, FG Trade, 17, fstop123, 8, kali9, 14, Liderina, Cover, Peter Cade, 7; Shutterstock: A Sharma, 16, Domira (background), cover and throughout, Halfpoint, 15, Hasnuddin, 11, Jesus Cervantes, 21, Kapitosh (cloud), cover and throughout, Kucher Serhii, 20, Marish (brave girl), cover and throughout, siro46, 13, Victoria Short, 20

Every effort has been made to contact copyright holders of material reproduced in this book. Any omissions will be rectified in subsequent printings if notice is given to the publisher.

All the internet addresses (URLs) given in this book were valid at the time of going to press. However, due to the dynamic nature of the internet, some addresses may have changed, or sites may have changed or ceased to exist since publication. While the author and publisher regret any inconvenience this may cause readers, no responsibility for any such changes can be accepted by either the author or the publisher.

Printed and bound in India.

CONTENTS

What is a friend?....................................4

Fears about friends...............................6

How to get started..............................10

Friendships over time 14

Showing friends you care 16

    Role-play making
    a new friend................................20

    Glossary 22

    Find out more 23

    Index..24

    About the author...........................24

Words in **bold** are in the glossary.

WHAT IS A FRIEND?

Friends are an important part of life. What is a friend? A friend is someone you enjoy being around. A friend is someone you can trust.

A friend will be there for you if you are feeling sad. A friend will laugh with you when you are feeling happy. Friends are with us in bad times. They are with us in good times. Friends make our lives better.

5

FEARS ABOUT FRIENDS

The thought of making new friends can be scary. This comes from a fear of **rejection**. You might worry that other people won't like you. You might worry that no one will want to play with you. It's okay to have these worries. Everyone has these feelings sometimes. You can push through the fear. You can be **brave**.

7

Thinking about making friends can cause you to worry about bullies. Some people have trouble being kind. They can say mean things. They can do mean things.

The good news is that the world has more kind people than bullies. Walk away from mean behaviour. Find someone kind instead.

HOW TO GET STARTED

It can feel **overwhelming** to make new friends. How should you begin? Think about something you know how to do well. Maybe it is drawing a picture of your family. Maybe it is singing your favourite song. You weren't perfect the first time you tried. But you kept trying!

11

New things take **practice**. It's the same way with friends. You can practise making new friends. You can **role-play** at home. Practise **introducing** yourself to someone new. It will help you feel more **confident**. You will not feel so afraid.

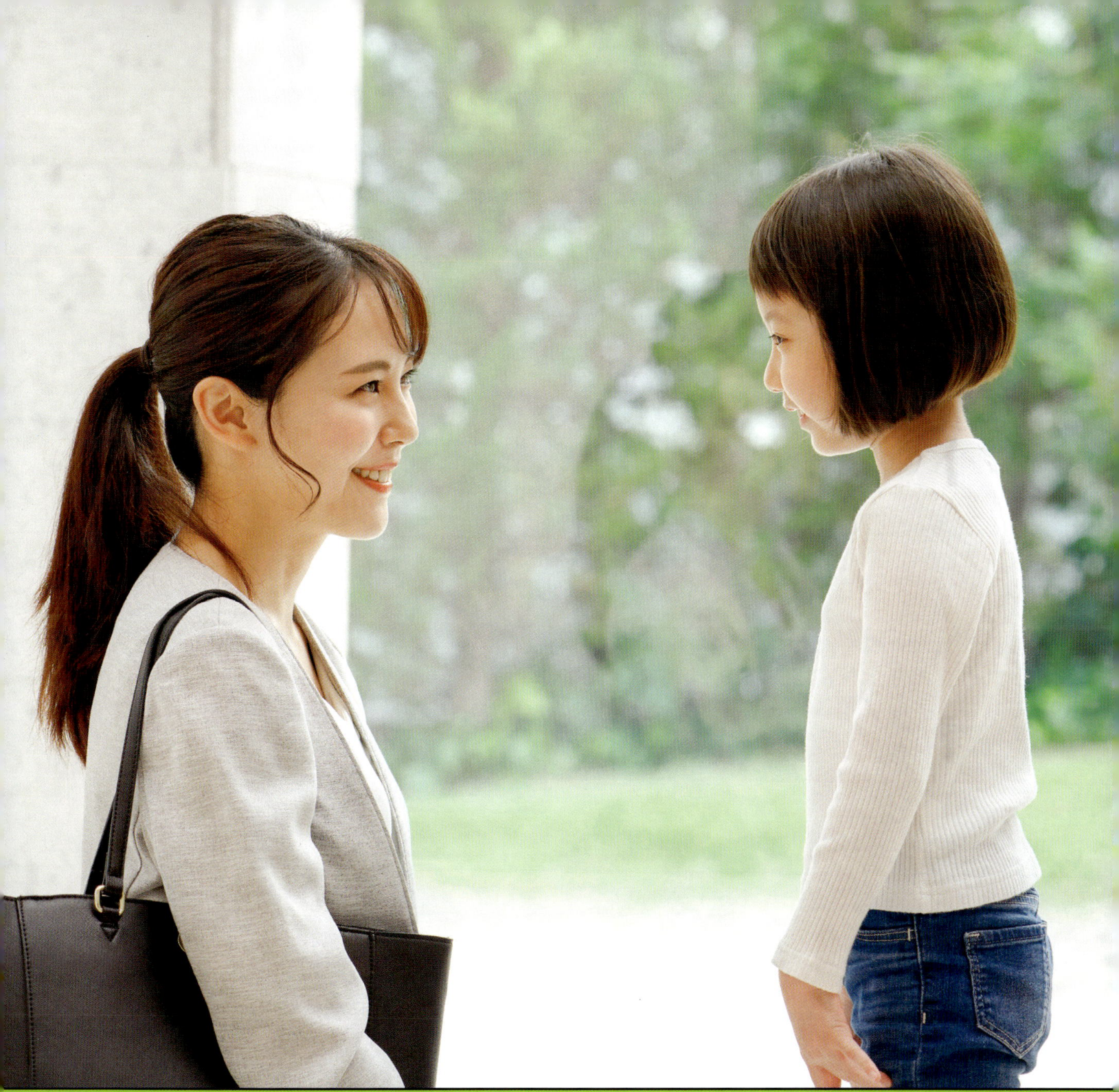

FRIENDSHIPS OVER TIME

Friendships don't always happen straight away. Start slowly. Introduce yourself. Tell new friends you are happy to see them. Ask if they want to play a game. Find out what they do for fun.

Friendships form over time. You will find things you have in common. You will learn how you are alike or different. Your friends don't have to be exactly like you. Each person is different and special.

15

SHOWING FRIENDS YOU CARE

It's important for you to be a good friend too. Show your friends you care about them. Be silly and make them laugh. Cheer them up when they are sad.

Remember we all make mistakes sometimes. We might say something unkind. We might not wait our turn. Say you are sorry. Ask for forgiveness. It's okay to make a mistake and move on.

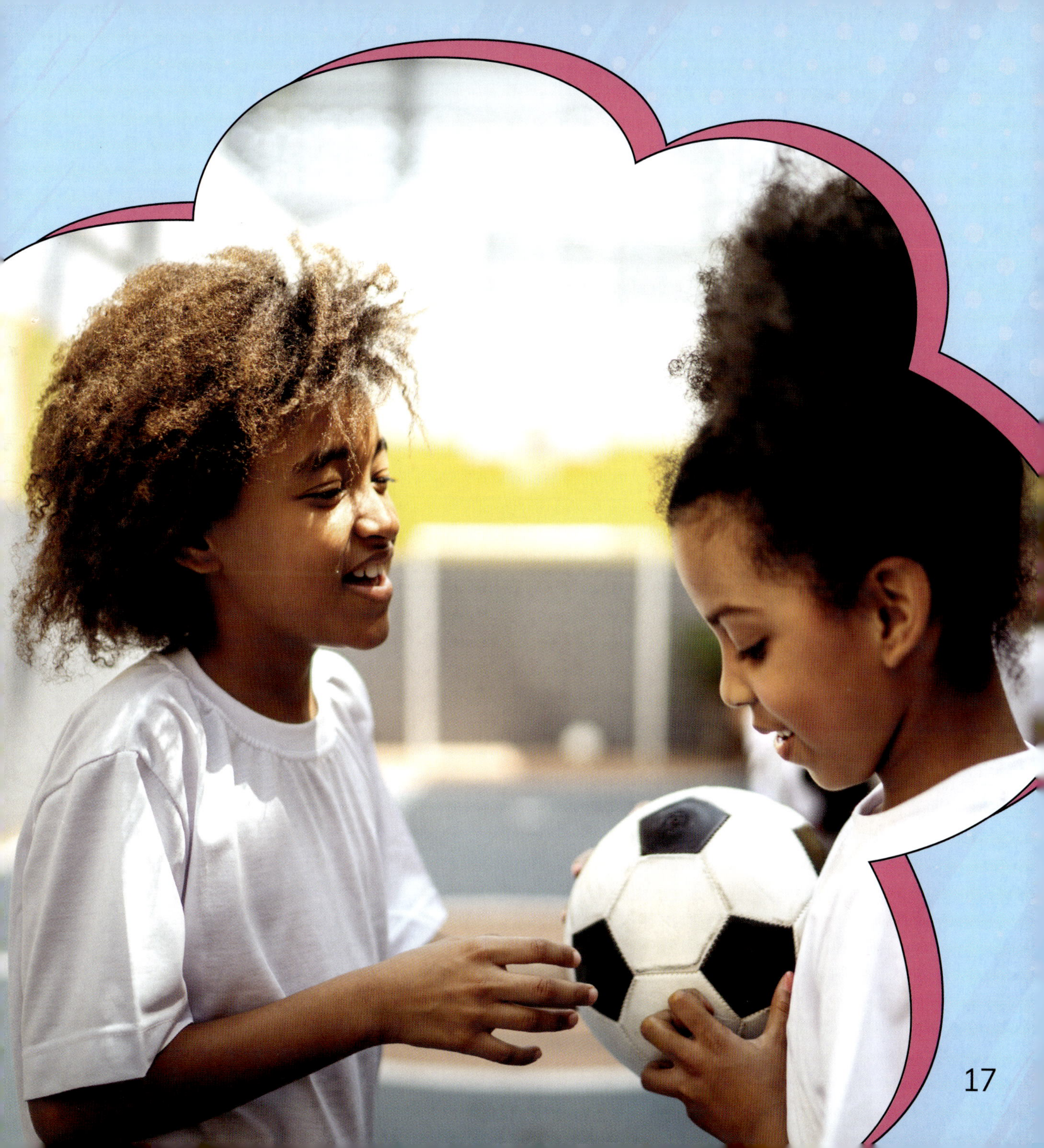

What if a friendship doesn't work out? That's okay! You don't have to be friends with everyone. You can look for new friends again. You can keep trying. The world is full of different people. You can make new friends everywhere.

19

ROLE-PLAY MAKING A NEW FRIEND

Practise introducing yourself to a new friend. This activity can help you know what to say when you meet someone new.

What you need

- coloured pencils or felt-tip pens
- index cards
- family member or a stuffed toy

What you do

1. Think about how to say hello. You can introduce yourself in many ways. Choose the way that feels most comfortable.

2. Write a script to help you remember what to say. Copy these lines onto the cards:

    Hi! My name is _____.

    What is your name?

    How are you today?

    It is nice to meet you!

20

3. Place a stuffed toy near you or find a family member to help.

4. Pretend you are talking to someone new. Tell yourself to be brave! Practise introducing yourself using your lines.

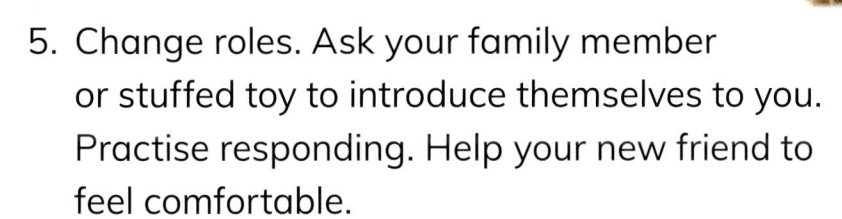

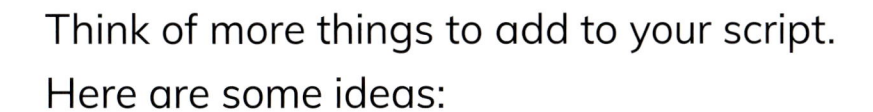

5. Change roles. Ask your family member or stuffed toy to introduce themselves to you. Practise responding. Help your new friend to feel comfortable.

Think of more things to add to your script. Here are some ideas:

Do you want to play a game?

Do you want to draw pictures with me?

What is your favourite animal?

Remember to practise more than once. The next time you meet someone new, use your lines to make a new friend!

GLOSSARY

brave willing to do difficult things even if you are scared

confident having the belief that you can do something well

introduce tell someone your name or the name of someone else when they are meeting for the first time

overwhelming very hard or difficult

practise keep working at improving a skill

rejection act of being left out or not accepted

role-play act in a scene with another person

FIND OUT MORE

Books

All About Friends, Felicity Brooks (Usborne, 2020)

Making Friends: A Book About First Friendships, Amanda McCardie (Walker Books, 2021)

Teach Your Dragon to Make Friends, Steve Herman (DG Books, 2018)

Websites

www.bbc.co.uk/bitesize/topics/zms6jhv/articles/zkgdcqt
This BBC Bitesize page will help you to deal with your feelings.

www.youtube.com/watch?v=ReMq3KX8F94
Watch this video to find out what makes a good friend.

INDEX

bullies 8, 9

forgiveness 16

introductions 12, 14

mistakes 16

practising 12

rejection 6

role-playing 12

trusting 4

trying 10, 18

worries 6, 8

ABOUT THE AUTHOR

Renee Biermann enjoys writing books for children. She has made many new friends in life. Even when she is afraid, she tries to make friends anyway. She lives in the United States with her two cats, Gretchen and Minou. Renee's cats are her friends too!